AI THAT PREDICTS GENE ACTIVITY IN ANY HUMAN CELL
The New Frontier of Science

How Artificial Intelligence is Unlocking the Hidden Worlds of Genetics and Technology

Tom E. Jackson

Table of Contents

Introduction

Hidden within the intricate threads of our DNA lies a mystery as profound and elusive as the cosmic dark matter that holds galaxies together. Just as astrophysicists have long puzzled over the unseen forces shaping the universe, scientists have struggled to unravel the secrets of the genome's so-called "dark matter"—vast stretches of non-coding DNA that were once dismissed as junk but now are suspected to hold the keys to many of life's deepest mysteries. These hidden regions influence everything from the activation of genes to the onset of diseases, yet their mechanisms have remained stubbornly out of reach.

Now, artificial intelligence has entered the picture, wielding tools powerful enough to illuminate the unseen. This is not just another step forward in scientific discovery—it is a leap into a new era where machines can predict, decode, and reveal what was previously unknowable. Imagine systems so advanced that they can forecast cellular behavior based on patterns buried deep in genetic data. Picture AI crafting blueprints for groundbreaking materials with the precision of a master artisan or analyzing X-rays with such accuracy that doctors are empowered to save lives faster than ever before.

This transformation is not limited to a single field. Across biology, material science, and medicine, artificial intelligence is rewriting the rules of what we can know and how quickly we can act on that knowledge. The convergence of human ingenuity and machine learning is no longer science fiction—it's the foundation of discoveries happening today. As the boundaries of science expand, so too does our ability to harness the unseen forces that shape our world, offering glimpses of a future where mysteries that have baffled humanity for generations are finally brought to light.

This journey begins with a single, audacious question: What happens when machines learn to see the invisible?

For centuries, science has been a practice of observation and description, capturing the intricacies of life, nature, and the universe as they appear. While this has led to groundbreaking discoveries, it has also limited our understanding to snapshots of what happens after the fact. We have analyzed the damaged mechanisms of diseased cells, observed the properties of materials long after their creation, and examined medical images with tools that can only interpret what already exists. The ability to foresee, to predict outcomes before they occur, has remained an elusive goal—until now.

Artificial intelligence is transforming this landscape, moving science from a reactive process to one that anticipates and predicts with astonishing accuracy. This shift is not just about speeding up existing processes; it's about unlocking new dimensions of understanding. In genetics, AI is helping us decipher the hidden grammar of our DNA, predicting how cells will behave and paving the way for targeted treatments. In material science, it's revolutionizing how we design and create, enabling the rapid discovery of advanced substances that could power the next wave of technological innovation. In medicine, AI is already enhancing diagnostic tools, reducing the time between detection and treatment in ways that could save countless lives.

This book explores these transformative breakthroughs in detail, beginning with the revolutionary strides in genetics that allow AI to predict gene activity in ways never before possible. It then delves into the world of materials discovery, where machine learning is accelerating the creation of vital substances for energy, medicine, and technology. Finally, it examines the remarkable advancements in radiology, showcasing how AI is reshaping medical imaging to deliver faster and more accurate diagnoses. Each chapter illuminates how these advancements are interconnected, showing the profound potential of AI to redefine science and its role in shaping humanity's future.

The journey ahead is one of discovery, innovation, and limitless possibility. By turning science into a predictive force, we are not just exploring the unknown—we are reshaping it. This is the story of how artificial intelligence is opening doors to a future once thought unimaginable, where the answers to life's greatest mysteries are no longer beyond our reach.

Chapter 1: AI in Genetics – Cracking the Code of Life

At Columbia University, a team of researchers led by Raul Rabadan achieved a breakthrough that could redefine the boundaries of modern biology. They developed an artificial intelligence system capable of predicting gene activity with unprecedented accuracy—a feat that traditional scientific methods have struggled to accomplish. This innovation represents a monumental leap forward, allowing scientists to move beyond observing cellular behavior after the fact and instead anticipate how cells might respond under varying conditions.

The AI system was designed to unravel the complexities of gene regulation, the intricate process that determines which genes are turned on or off in any given cell. This process is central to how cells function, adapt, and respond to external stimuli, yet it is governed by an elaborate and often unpredictable interplay of factors. By leveraging vast amounts of data—over 1.3 million human cells—the AI was trained to recognize patterns that elude even the most advanced experimental techniques.

Much like a linguist learning the structure and syntax of a new language, the AI has mastered the grammar of the genome. It deciphers how different segments of DNA interact and how those interactions dictate the activation or suppression of specific genes. The implications are staggering: this system can now predict gene activity in virtually any type of cell, whether healthy or diseased, even in cases it has never encountered before. This ability to generalize and apply its knowledge to unfamiliar scenarios sets it apart from previous models and marks a significant step toward turning biology into a predictive science.

Rabadan and his team have essentially built a foundation for understanding cellular behavior in a way that was previously unimaginable. The AI not only opens doors to studying existing cellular processes but also creates opportunities to explore how cells might respond to entirely new stimuli or mutations. This is not a tool for merely cataloging what is already known; it is an instrument for uncovering the unknown.

The foundation of this revolutionary AI system lies in its ability to learn from an immense dataset: 1.3 million human cells, each carrying its unique genetic blueprint. This vast reservoir of information provided the raw material for the AI to decode the complex patterns that govern gene regulation. By analyzing the interactions between different segments of DNA and their associated proteins, the AI began to uncover the underlying rules that dictate when and how specific genes are activated or suppressed.

To understand its approach, imagine teaching a machine to grasp the nuances of a language. Much like how AI models such as ChatGPT analyze billions of sentences to learn the structure, syntax, and rules of human language, this system absorbed the intricate "grammar" of the genome. It learned to identify which segments of DNA interact, how those interactions influence gene expression, and how accessibility to these genetic regions shapes cellular behavior.

This process was not about memorizing isolated instances. Instead, the AI identified patterns and relationships that repeat across various cell types and conditions. It became adept at recognizing the subtle regulatory cues that guide gene activity, much like understanding how context determines the meaning of a word in a sentence. These insights allowed the system to generalize its predictions, accurately forecasting gene activity in new cell types it had never been trained on.

The real genius of this approach lies in its predictive power. By internalizing the "rules" of genetic grammar, the AI can now be presented with a completely unfamiliar cell type—one it has no prior knowledge of—and predict with remarkable accuracy which genes will be active. This capability bridges a critical gap in biology, moving beyond descriptive observation to predictive insight, enabling researchers to explore questions that were once out of reach.

Predicting gene activity is more than a scientific curiosity; it is a transformative leap in how we understand and address the complexities of life. Traditionally, biology has been a descriptive science, focused on observing and cataloging what happens after a cellular process has unfolded. While these observations have provided valuable insights, they often leave scientists grappling with the question of *why* certain behaviors occur or *how* they might change under different conditions.

The ability to predict gene activity shifts the narrative entirely. Instead of merely describing how a cell behaves when it is exposed to a particular environment or mutation, researchers can now anticipate these responses before they occur. This foresight opens new dimensions in understanding cellular behavior, allowing scientists to simulate and test scenarios that were previously inaccessible. It is akin to reading the script of a play before it is performed, offering the chance to rewrite problematic scenes before they play out.

This predictive capability is especially crucial when it comes to diseases caused by gene mutations. Many conditions, such as cancer, are rooted in disruptions to the normal regulation of gene activity. Mutations can alter how genes are switched on or off, leading to cascading effects that drive the development of abnormal cells. By predicting which genes will be affected by a specific mutation, scientists can pinpoint the underlying mechanisms that fuel these diseases.

Take, for instance, inherited conditions like pediatric leukemia. Understanding how a single mutation can disrupt cellular regulation allows researchers to identify the critical pathways involved and target them with precision therapies. Instead of treating symptoms or broadly targeting affected tissues, medicine can become more personalized and efficient, focusing directly on the disrupted processes.

Moreover, predicting gene activity has the potential to illuminate the vast, uncharted regions of the genome often referred to as "dark matter." These non-coding regions, while not directly involved in protein production, play a critical role in regulating gene expression. Most mutations linked to cancer lie within these areas, yet their effects have remained largely mysterious. With AI's predictive power, scientists can now begin to understand how changes in these hidden regions influence cellular behavior, providing new targets for treatment and unlocking a deeper understanding of human biology.

By turning biology from a descriptive to a predictive science, this breakthrough not only expands the horizons of research but also lays the groundwork for a future where diseases can be anticipated, intercepted, and potentially prevented before they ever manifest.

One of the most compelling demonstrations of this AI's capabilities lies in its application to pediatric leukemia, a devastating condition that arises from inherited genetic mutations. For years, scientists knew that children with a particular mutation were at heightened risk of developing leukemia, but the precise mechanism driving the disease remained elusive. The AI provided the breakthrough needed to connect the dots.

By analyzing genetic data, the system predicted that the mutation disrupted the interaction between two critical transcription factors. These are specialized proteins responsible for regulating which genes are turned on or off within a cell. In this case, the AI uncovered that the mutation rerouted these transcription factors, leading to abnormal gene expression that fueled the unchecked growth of leukemia cells. This insight revealed a previously hidden mechanism underlying the disease.

What made this breakthrough even more remarkable was the validation it received in the lab.

Researchers conducted experiments to test the AI's predictions, confirming that the disrupted interaction was indeed at the heart of the issue. The AI's ability to pinpoint the specific regulatory breakdown provided a clear target for potential treatments—something that had eluded researchers relying solely on traditional methods.

With this knowledge, the door opened to developing therapies aimed at restoring normal transcription factor interactions. By targeting the precise pathways disrupted by the mutation, scientists can work on treatments that are more focused and effective, reducing the collateral damage often associated with broad-spectrum approaches. This targeted strategy holds the promise of not only improving outcomes for patients but also minimizing side effects, especially critical in treating children.

This case exemplifies how AI's predictive power can go beyond theoretical insights to drive actionable results. It showcases the potential for this technology to revolutionize not just our understanding of diseases but also the way we approach their treatment, paving the way for a future of personalized and precise medicine.

Deep within the human genome lies a vast expanse of DNA that doesn't code for proteins, a mysterious region once dismissed as "junk DNA." Today, this so-called genomic "dark matter" is recognized as anything but useless. These non-coding regions, which make up the majority of our DNA, play a pivotal role in regulating gene expression. They act as switches, silencers, and enhancers, dictating when and where specific genes are activated. However, their complexity and subtlety have made them one of biology's most enigmatic frontiers.

This is where AI is proving transformative. Unlike protein-coding genes, which are relatively well-mapped, the regulatory sequences hidden within non-coding DNA are notoriously difficult to study. Traditional approaches struggle to untangle their intricate interactions or predict how

17

mutations in these regions might affect gene activity. AI, with its ability to sift through massive datasets and identify patterns invisible to the human eye, is uniquely suited to explore this uncharted territory.

One of the most significant discoveries emerging from this work is the realization that many cancer-related mutations reside in these non-coding regions. While they may not directly disrupt a protein, they can alter the switches that control gene expression, leading to misregulated cellular behavior. For example, a mutation in an enhancer sequence might cause an oncogene—a gene associated with cancer growth—to remain perpetually active. Until now, understanding the impact of these mutations was an immense challenge.

With its predictive capabilities, AI can illuminate these hidden regions, identifying which mutations in non-coding DNA might lead to changes in gene expression. By simulating how these alterations disrupt normal cellular processes, researchers can better understand the root causes of genetic diseases, particularly those like cancer that often originate in these regulatory networks.

The implications extend far beyond oncology. Many genetic disorders, from neurodevelopmental conditions to autoimmune diseases, are influenced by mutations in non-coding regions. By providing a roadmap to explore these previously inaccessible areas of the genome, AI is enabling a deeper understanding of how our DNA operates as a whole. It allows researchers to bridge the gap between genetic changes and their downstream effects, creating new opportunities for early detection, precise diagnostics, and targeted interventions.

This newfound ability to decode the genomic "dark matter" is more than a scientific milestone—it's a paradigm shift. By shedding light on these hidden areas, AI is not only unraveling the mysteries of our DNA but also offering new hope for tackling diseases that were once thought to be beyond our reach.

Chapter 2: MatterGen – AI in Materials Science

The story of human progress is inseparably tied to the materials we have discovered and mastered. From the Stone Age to the Information Age, the development of new materials has shaped civilizations, transformed industries, and defined eras. Steel, for instance, revolutionized construction and infrastructure, enabling the rise of skyscrapers and railways. Silicon ushered in the digital age, powering everything from computers to smartphones and fundamentally altering the way humans interact with the world.

Despite these transformative advancements, the discovery of new materials has always been a slow and painstaking process. Traditional methods rely heavily on trial and error, requiring scientists to sift through countless combinations of elements and compounds in search of materials with the desired properties. Each candidate must be synthesized, tested, and analyzed—a labor-intensive cycle that can take years, if not decades, to yield results.

The complexity of this challenge grows with the demands of modern technology. Today, we need materials that are not only efficient but also sustainable, durable, and capable of performing under extreme conditions. Whether it's creating longer-lasting batteries for electric vehicles, developing superconductors for quantum computing, or designing polymers for advanced medical devices, the bar is higher than ever.

Yet, as the need for innovation accelerates, the traditional approach to materials discovery struggles to keep pace. The cost of experimentation is staggering, both in terms of time and resources. Laboratories are constrained by physical and chemical limitations, unable to test more than a fraction of the possibilities within the vast universe of potential materials. This bottleneck has left entire industries yearning for a faster, more efficient way to uncover the building blocks of the future.

The limitations of conventional methods highlight the urgent need for a breakthrough—one that could redefine how we search for and design materials. It is in this context that artificial intelligence enters the picture, offering a transformative approach to material science that could save years of labor and bring us closer to solutions that once seemed out of reach.

Enter MatterGen, a revolutionary AI system poised to transform the way we discover and design materials. At its core, MatterGen operates like a "text-to-image" model, but instead of creating visual representations, it crafts molecular blueprints for new materials based on specific desired properties. This approach combines the creativity of generative AI with the precision of material science, offering a faster and more efficient path to innovation.

The process begins with a simple yet profound question: What properties should the material have? Scientists input these specifications into MatterGen, detailing characteristics such as conductivity, durability, heat resistance, or energy efficiency. For instance, they might request a material that can hold a battery charge for an extended period while remaining stable at high temperatures. With this input, the AI gets to work.

MatterGen analyzes the vast universe of potential compounds and molecular structures, drawing on its training to generate a blueprint tailored to meet the requested properties. Unlike traditional methods, which rely on labor-intensive experimentation, MatterGen skips the guesswork by focusing only on the most promising candidates. It offers designs that are not just theoretical but practical, bridging the gap between concept and reality.

Once the AI generates a blueprint, researchers synthesize the material in the lab and test its properties. In early trials, the first material created using MatterGen's design came remarkably close to the targeted specifications—within 20% of the requested values. This level of accuracy on a first attempt demonstrates the system's potential to drastically reduce the time and effort required for materials discovery.

This streamlined process—defining properties, generating blueprints, and testing materials—represents a profound shift. Where it once took years to explore even a narrow subset of possibilities, MatterGen allows researchers to move at an unprecedented pace. It doesn't just improve efficiency; it opens the door to exploring new materials that might otherwise have been overlooked, accelerating progress in fields ranging from sustainable energy to advanced computing.

MatterGen is more than a tool; it's a visionary leap forward, transforming the way scientists approach the building blocks of innovation. By turning ideas into actionable designs, it bridges the gap between imagination and reality, setting the stage for a new era of material science.

The early successes of MatterGen offer a glimpse into the transformative potential of AI-driven materials discovery. In one notable example, researchers tasked the AI with designing a material that met a specific set of properties, such as stability, conductivity, and durability. Using its vast understanding of molecular interactions, MatterGen generated a blueprint for a compound that had never been synthesized before. When scientists brought the design to life in the lab, the material's properties came astonishingly close to the target—falling within just 20% of the desired values. For a first attempt, this level of accuracy was groundbreaking.

This success underscores the immense promise of AI in an area that has traditionally relied on painstaking trial and error. In conventional materials science, researchers might spend years testing countless combinations of elements and structures, often with no guarantee of finding a viable solution. Each iteration requires synthesis, analysis, and refinement, creating a bottleneck that limits the pace of innovation. MatterGen disrupts this paradigm by drastically narrowing the search, providing scientists with blueprints that are already optimized for success.

The implications extend far beyond just saving time. By reducing the trial-and-error process, MatterGen also minimizes resource consumption, cutting the cost of materials research. This efficiency enables scientists to explore a wider range of possibilities, delving into areas that might have previously been deemed too time-intensive or expensive to investigate. Entire industries, from energy to healthcare, stand to benefit as new materials are developed faster and more economically than ever before.

Perhaps most importantly, MatterGen's early success demonstrates the scalability of its approach. As the system continues to learn and refine its capabilities, its predictions are likely to become even more precise. This means that the next generation of materials—whether for renewable energy, quantum computing, or medical devices—could emerge not in decades, but in a matter of years. By turning what was once an unpredictable process into a streamlined, data-driven endeavor, MatterGen is redefining the boundaries of possibility in material science.

MatterGen's potential extends far beyond its efficiency in material discovery—it holds the power to reshape entire industries through its transformative applications. By addressing critical challenges in fields like energy, computing, and medicine, this AI-driven tool is accelerating progress toward solutions that could define the future.

One of the most pressing demands of the modern era lies in sustainable energy. Electric vehicles (EVs) have emerged as a cornerstone of the transition to greener transportation, but their widespread adoption hinges on better battery technology. Current batteries often struggle with limited capacity, slow charging times, and performance degradation over time. MatterGen provides a way forward by designing advanced materials that can enhance battery performance. For instance, it can create materials capable of holding a charge for longer durations, maintaining stability at extreme temperatures, or supporting rapid recharging cycles. These breakthroughs could lead to lighter, more efficient batteries, enabling EVs to travel greater distances while reducing their environmental impact.

In the realm of quantum computing, MatterGen offers a solution to one of the field's most significant hurdles: the need for superconducting materials. Superconductors, which allow electricity to flow without resistance, are critical for building powerful and efficient quantum processors. However, existing superconducting materials often require extremely low temperatures to function, making them expensive and challenging to use. MatterGen's ability to design new superconductors with enhanced properties—such as higher critical temperatures or improved stability—could revolutionize quantum computing. These advancements would pave the way for practical, scalable quantum technologies, unlocking computational power far beyond the capabilities of classical computers.

Medicine is another arena where MatterGen's influence is poised to make a profound impact. Medical devices and treatments increasingly rely on specialized polymers, which need to be tailored for specific functions. Whether it's a polymer that can safely deliver drugs to a targeted area of the body or a biocompatible material for advanced prosthetics, the requirements for these materials are exacting. MatterGen can streamline the creation of such polymers, ensuring they meet precise criteria while reducing the time and cost of development. This could lead to more effective treatments, improved patient outcomes, and innovative medical technologies that were previously out of reach.

These transformative applications highlight MatterGen's role as a catalyst for innovation. By breaking through the barriers of traditional material discovery, it is not only solving existing challenges but also enabling entirely new possibilities. From cleaner energy solutions to cutting-edge technology and life-saving medical advancements, MatterGen is shaping a future where the limits of what we can create are defined only by our imagination.

Chapter 3: RadDino – Revolutionizing Radiology

Radiology has long been a cornerstone of modern medicine, offering a window into the human body through imaging techniques like X-rays, CT scans, and MRIs. These tools allow physicians to detect conditions ranging from fractures to tumors, often serving as the first step in diagnosis and treatment. However, the field faces significant challenges that can hinder its effectiveness, particularly in high-pressure environments like emergency rooms.

One of the greatest obstacles in radiology is the sheer volume of images that must be analyzed. Modern imaging technologies generate a wealth of data, and interpreting these images requires meticulous attention to detail. Radiologists must identify subtle anomalies, track changes over time, and compare findings across multiple scans—a process that is both time-intensive and mentally taxing. The complexity increases further in cases where images must be cross-referenced with patient histories or prior reports, making the workload even more daunting.

In emergency situations, where every second counts, these challenges become even more pronounced. A patient arriving with symptoms of a stroke, internal injury, or respiratory distress needs immediate attention, and delays in analyzing their medical images can have life-altering consequences. While radiologists are highly trained experts, human limitations such as fatigue or the risk of oversight can slow down the process or lead to missed details.

This is where artificial intelligence has the potential to redefine the landscape of medical imaging. By automating key aspects of image analysis, AI can address the bottlenecks that radiologists face, offering faster and more accurate interpretations. For emergencies, this means critical anomalies—such as internal bleeding, misplaced catheters, or signs of disease progression—can be flagged almost instantaneously. Instead of spending valuable time sifting through images, clinicians can focus on forming treatment plans and saving lives.

The role of AI in radiology is not to replace human expertise but to enhance it. By serving as an assistive tool, AI can handle repetitive and data-heavy tasks, freeing radiologists to focus on complex cases that require their judgment and insight. This partnership between humans and machines has the potential to transform radiology into a more efficient, precise, and responsive discipline, meeting the growing demands of modern healthcare while delivering better outcomes for patients.

The RadDino system, developed in collaboration with the Mayo Clinic, represents a new era in medical imaging. This advanced AI tool combines the power of image analysis with natural language processing to deliver a comprehensive approach to radiology. By integrating these capabilities, RadDino doesn't just interpret X-rays visually; it also reads and analyzes associated radiology reports, enabling it to identify anomalies with remarkable precision.

What sets RadDino apart is its ability to bridge two critical aspects of radiology: detecting patterns in medical images and understanding the context provided by accompanying medical text. For example, when processing a chest X-ray, the system doesn't only highlight visible abnormalities like a shadow on the lung or a misplaced catheter. It also cross-references these findings with the patient's history and prior reports to detect patterns or changes that might not be immediately apparent. This dual-layered analysis provides a more complete picture, reducing the likelihood of oversight.

The collaboration with the Mayo Clinic ensures that RadDino operates at the highest standard of accuracy and reliability. The system has been trained on vast datasets of X-ray images and radiology reports, enabling it to learn from real-world examples. This rigorous development process ensures that its outputs are not only clinically relevant but also aligned with the demands of medical professionals.

RadDino's text analysis capabilities are particularly significant. Radiologists often rely on detailed written reports to convey nuanced findings, and these documents can contain critical information that might not be evident in the image alone. By analyzing both the text and the image, RadDino can correlate findings, highlight inconsistencies, or flag potential issues for further review. For instance, if an X-ray shows a slight abnormality that was previously noted but unchanged, RadDino can confirm stability. Conversely, if the anomaly has grown or worsened, the system will prioritize it for urgent attention.

This seamless integration of text and image analysis positions RadDino as an invaluable partner in modern radiology. It not only speeds up the diagnostic process but also enhances accuracy, ensuring that even subtle changes or hard-to-spot issues are brought to light. For patients, this means quicker diagnoses and more targeted treatment plans, particularly in time-sensitive scenarios. For radiologists, it offers a tool that complements their expertise, allowing them to focus on the most complex and critical cases. Together, RadDino and its human counterparts are reshaping the future of medical imaging.

RadDino is more than just an analytical tool; it is a game-changer for hospital workflows, particularly in high-pressure environments where efficiency and accuracy are paramount. By harnessing its ability to analyze both medical images and textual reports, RadDino can quickly flag critical issues that might otherwise require meticulous and time-consuming manual review. This streamlining of the diagnostic process frees up valuable time for clinicians and radiologists, allowing them to focus on more complex decision-making and patient care.

Take, for example, the challenge of detecting subtle anomalies or errors in medical imaging. A catheter placed incorrectly during an emergency procedure might not always be immediately obvious, particularly if the radiologist is managing multiple urgent cases. RadDino excels at identifying such issues, using its deep learning algorithms to highlight areas of concern. Whether it's an incorrectly positioned tube, a shadow that warrants further investigation, or an emerging change in a lesion, the system ensures these details are brought to the forefront quickly and reliably.

One of RadDino's standout features is its ability to provide pre-analyzed reports. Instead of radiologists starting from scratch with each new image, the system offers an initial assessment that includes flagged areas, context from prior scans, and possible patterns of progression. For instance, if a chest X-ray shows worsening fluid buildup compared to a previous scan, RadDino will not only highlight this but also provide textual context, noting the trend over time. This synthesis of data means radiologists can confirm or refine the system's findings instead of spending hours manually reviewing every detail.

By automating routine tasks and pre-analyzing reports, RadDino reduces the risk of human error while lightening the workload on clinicians. This is especially valuable in emergency rooms or intensive care units, where rapid decisions can mean the difference between life and death. A patient arriving with respiratory distress, for example, could have their X-ray analyzed by RadDino within minutes, with flagged concerns and a summarized report ready for immediate review. This accelerates the diagnostic process, ensuring that treatment can begin as quickly as possible.

The ripple effects of these efficiencies extend beyond radiology departments. Faster diagnostics mean patients can be moved through the care system more swiftly, reducing bottlenecks and improving hospital-wide resource allocation. From time-sensitive emergencies to routine imaging, RadDino is transforming workflows, making healthcare faster, safer, and more effective for everyone involved.

RadDino's success with X-ray analysis is only the beginning of what AI can achieve in medical imaging. The future possibilities are vast, with opportunities to expand its capabilities to more advanced imaging techniques like CT scans and MRIs. These modalities, which generate even more detailed and complex datasets, stand to benefit immensely from AI's ability to analyze patterns and synthesize insights at unparalleled speed and accuracy.

CT scans, for example, often involve hundreds of cross-sectional images that require careful examination to detect subtle changes or anomalies. In cases of trauma or internal injury, where quick decisions are critical, an AI system like RadDino could provide rapid pre-analysis, highlighting areas of concern and cross-referencing them with patient histories. Similarly, MRIs, which are often used to visualize soft tissues, could benefit from AI's precision in identifying early signs of conditions like tumors or neurodegenerative diseases. By integrating these capabilities, RadDino could become an all-encompassing diagnostic tool, reducing the burden on radiologists while ensuring no detail is overlooked.

Beyond imaging, the potential for AI to create a seamless diagnostic process in healthcare is transformative. Imagine a future where a patient's journey through the diagnostic phase is fully integrated and optimized. From the moment an image is taken, AI systems could analyze it, compare it with previous scans, integrate findings with electronic medical records, and generate a comprehensive report—all within minutes. This could include not just identifying abnormalities but also predicting their progression, suggesting potential diagnoses, and even recommending follow-up tests or treatments.

Such a system could revolutionize how healthcare providers deliver care, especially in resource-strapped environments. In rural or underserved areas where access to specialists is limited, AI could serve as an expert second opinion, ensuring patients receive accurate and timely diagnoses. It could also alleviate the pressure on overburdened hospitals, allowing radiologists to focus on cases requiring their expertise while routine imaging is handled by AI.

As these technologies evolve, the possibilities extend even further. AI could one day be used to identify patterns across population-level data, spotting trends that could inform public health strategies or early detection programs for widespread conditions. For individual patients, the integration of AI into imaging and diagnostics could lead to more personalized care, tailoring treatments based on predictive insights unique to each case.

The future of medical imaging is one where AI plays a central role, not as a replacement for human expertise but as a powerful ally. By expanding its reach to other imaging techniques and integrating seamlessly into diagnostic workflows, RadDino and systems like it have the potential to redefine healthcare as we know it, making it faster, more precise, and more accessible to all.

Chapter 4: Ethical Considerations and Challenges

As artificial intelligence becomes an integral part of healthcare, the quality of the data used to train these systems takes on critical importance. High-quality training data is the foundation upon which AI models are built. Without accurate, diverse, and representative datasets, even the most advanced algorithms risk producing unreliable or skewed results, particularly in sensitive areas like medical imaging and diagnostics.

AI models like RadDino rely on vast amounts of medical images and associated reports to learn and improve their performance. These datasets must cover a wide range of cases, patient demographics, and imaging scenarios to ensure the AI can generalize its findings effectively. For example, a robust training dataset would include images from patients of different ages, genders, ethnicities, and health conditions. This diversity is essential for ensuring the model can accurately analyze images from any patient population it encounters.

However, when training data lacks this diversity, the risk of bias emerges. If an AI system is primarily trained on data from one demographic group, it may perform poorly when analyzing images from patients outside that group. In healthcare, this can have serious consequences, leading to disparities in diagnosis and treatment. For instance, studies have shown that AI systems trained predominantly on data from lighter-skinned individuals can struggle to detect conditions on darker skin tones, potentially resulting in missed diagnoses for those patients.

Bias in AI systems can also arise from subtle flaws in how data is labeled or processed. Radiology reports, for example, may reflect the subjective judgments of individual radiologists, introducing inconsistencies that the AI might inadvertently learn. These biases can compound over time, especially in high-stakes environments like healthcare, where precision is paramount.

Addressing these challenges requires a commitment to transparency and rigor in the development of AI models. Researchers must carefully curate training datasets to ensure they are as inclusive and representative as possible. Additionally, models should be rigorously tested on independent datasets to verify their performance across diverse populations and clinical scenarios.

Beyond the data itself, developers must remain vigilant about how these systems are implemented in real-world settings. Continuous monitoring and auditing are essential to identify and correct biases that might emerge after deployment. By prioritizing fairness, accountability, and inclusivity, AI in healthcare can live up to its promise of improving outcomes for all patients, not just a select few.

While the potential of AI in healthcare is immense, its success depends on the integrity of the data it learns from. High-quality, unbiased datasets are not just a technical requirement; they are a moral imperative in ensuring that these tools benefit everyone equally, bridging gaps in care rather than widening them.

As artificial intelligence becomes increasingly woven into the fabric of healthcare, the importance of safety and reliability cannot be overstated. AI systems like RadDino hold immense promise, but their deployment in real-world medical environments must be approached with caution to ensure patient safety and uphold the highest standards of ethical medical practice. Rigorous testing and validation are key components of this process.

Before any AI model is implemented in a clinical setting, it must undergo extensive testing to confirm its accuracy, consistency, and reliability. This involves subjecting the model to a wide range of scenarios using diverse datasets that reflect real-world conditions. For instance, an AI designed for radiology should be tested across different imaging techniques, equipment, patient demographics, and clinical settings to ensure its predictions hold up under varying circumstances. Models must also demonstrate robustness in detecting rare or complex conditions, as these cases often present the greatest challenges in healthcare.

Validation doesn't stop at accuracy. AI systems must also be evaluated for their ability to provide actionable and interpretable insights. In a medical context, it's not enough for the AI to flag an anomaly—it must do so in a way that aligns with the workflows and decision-making processes of healthcare providers. For example, RadDino's predictions must integrate seamlessly into radiologists' reports, offering clear, evidence-backed observations that clinicians can trust and act upon.

Ethical considerations play a central role in ensuring AI aligns with the principles of medicine. Predictions generated by AI must be free from biases that could lead to inequitable outcomes or misdiagnoses. Developers and healthcare institutions must also prioritize transparency, ensuring clinicians understand how the system arrives at its conclusions. This fosters trust and allows human experts to verify or challenge AI-generated insights as needed.

Safety protocols must also account for the fact that no system, AI included, is infallible. Mechanisms should be in place to identify and correct errors quickly, minimizing any potential harm to patients. Continuous monitoring of AI performance is essential, particularly as new data and use cases emerge. This includes post-deployment audits to assess whether the system is performing as intended and whether updates or retraining are needed to maintain its reliability.

Finally, AI in healthcare must always complement, not replace, human expertise. While tools like RadDino can enhance efficiency and accuracy, they are designed to support clinicians, not make independent decisions. By maintaining a collaborative relationship between humans and machines, the healthcare system can leverage the strengths of AI while preserving the vital role of medical professionals in ensuring patient safety.

In a field as critical as healthcare, the stakes are too high for shortcuts or oversights. By prioritizing rigorous testing, transparency, and ethical considerations, AI can be deployed safely and reliably, fulfilling its potential to transform medicine without compromising the trust and well-being of patients.

Transparency and trust are foundational to the successful integration of artificial intelligence into healthcare. While the capabilities of AI systems like RadDino are impressive, their adoption hinges on the confidence of researchers, practitioners, and patients alike. For AI to fulfill its promise in medicine, it must not only produce accurate results but also do so in a way that is clear, interpretable, and supportive of human expertise.

One of the primary challenges lies in the explainability of AI models. Many advanced systems operate as "black boxes," producing outputs without revealing the underlying logic behind their predictions. In healthcare, this opacity can be problematic. A radiologist, for example, must understand why RadDino flagged a particular anomaly in an X-ray to confidently integrate that insight into their diagnosis. Without a clear rationale, even the most accurate predictions can feel unreliable or difficult to trust.

To address this, researchers are working to make AI models more interpretable. This involves developing systems that not only deliver results but also explain the steps they took to reach their conclusions. For instance, RadDino might highlight specific areas of an image, detail the patterns it detected, and correlate those findings with similar cases in its training data. By providing this level of transparency, the AI fosters trust and allows medical professionals to validate its outputs against their own expertise.

Another key aspect of building trust is addressing fears about the role of AI in replacing human expertise. The idea of machines taking over critical tasks in medicine can spark concerns about job displacement, loss of control, and even ethical decision-making. However, the reality is far more collaborative. AI systems are designed to enhance human capabilities, not replace them. RadDino, for instance, acts as a powerful assistant, handling repetitive tasks and flagging potential issues so radiologists can focus on complex and nuanced cases.

Emphasizing this collaborative relationship can help alleviate fears and demonstrate the value of AI as a tool for empowerment rather than replacement. For example, in a high-pressure emergency room setting, AI's ability to rapidly analyze images can complement a physician's decision-making, ensuring no time is lost in critical moments. Rather than diminishing the role of healthcare professionals, AI allows them to work more efficiently and effectively, ultimately improving patient outcomes.

Transparency also extends to patients, who must trust that AI-driven systems are being used responsibly and ethically. Hospitals and developers can build this trust by openly sharing how these systems are trained, validated, and monitored for fairness and reliability. Providing clear communication about the role of AI in patient care helps to demystify the technology and ensures that patients feel informed and confident in their treatment.

By prioritizing explainability, collaboration, and open communication, the healthcare system can foster trust in AI technologies. This trust is essential for unlocking the full potential of AI, allowing it to work hand-in-hand with human expertise to deliver safer, faster, and more effective care.

Conclusion

Artificial intelligence is reshaping the boundaries of science in ways that were once unimaginable, marking a pivotal moment in human history. Across diverse fields—genetics, materials science, and radiology—AI is transforming how we understand, innovate, and act. By moving from a descriptive to a predictive model, it has unlocked doors that have long remained closed, illuminating mysteries within the genome, accelerating the creation of advanced materials, and redefining how we approach medical diagnostics.

In genetics, AI has demonstrated the ability to predict gene activity and unravel the intricacies of the genome's dark matter. This advancement has already led to breakthroughs, such as understanding the mechanisms behind pediatric leukemia and offering new avenues for targeted therapies. In materials science, AI systems like MatterGen have accelerated the discovery process, designing advanced materials for sustainable energy, quantum computing, and medical applications with unprecedented speed and precision. Meanwhile, in radiology, tools like RadDino are enhancing diagnostic workflows, flagging anomalies, and supporting faster, more accurate decisions in life-critical situations.

Looking forward, the possibilities are as vast as they are exciting. AI is poised to play a central role in fields like drug discovery, where it could significantly reduce the time needed to identify and develop new treatments. Its predictive power may lead to more personalized medicine, tailoring interventions to the unique genetic and biological makeup of individual patients. Beyond healthcare, AI has the potential to revolutionize climate science, robotics, and countless other domains, driving innovations that could fundamentally change how we live and interact with the world.

But perhaps the most profound aspect of AI is its ability to act as a true partner in scientific discovery. It is not merely a tool that enhances efficiency; it is an ally capable of solving problems and uncovering patterns that have eluded us for generations. By working alongside human ingenuity, AI enables us to explore the unknown, turning complex challenges into solvable puzzles and pushing the boundaries of what we can achieve.

As we stand on the threshold of this new era, the potential of AI to unlock the secrets of life and the universe is boundless. It is a reminder that innovation is not an endpoint but a continuous journey—one that promises to take humanity further than we've ever gone before. This partnership between humans and machines is not just reshaping science; it is redefining what it means to discover, to create, and to understand.